Reading Street

Program Authors

Peter Afflerbach

Camille Blachowicz

Candy Dawson Boyd

Elena Izquierdo

Connie Juel

Edward Kame'enui

Donald Leu

Jeanne R. Paratore

P. David Pearson

Sam Sebesta

Deborah Simmons

Alfred Tatum

Sharon Vaughn

Susan Watts Taffe

Karen Kring Wixson

PEARSON

Glenview, Illinois • Boston, Massachusetts • Chandler, Arizona •
Upper Saddle River, New Jersey

We dedicate Reading Street to
Peter Jovanovich.

His wisdom, courage,
and passion for education
are an inspiration to us all.

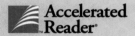

About the Cover Artist
Rob Hefferan likes to reminisce about the simple life he had as a child growing up in Cheshire, when his biggest worry was whether to have fish fingers or Alphabetti Spaghetti for tea. The faces, colors, and shapes from that time are a present-day inspiration for his artwork.

ISBN-13: 978-0-328-48108-8
ISBN-10:   0-328-48108-4
7 8 9 10 V011 14 13 12 11
CC1

Dear Reader,

Hold on to your thinking caps! Our next trip on Reading Street is all about adventure! We will see the world with a rooster, travel to the coldest place on Earth, and fly over New York City. Are you ready?

AlphaBuddy says, "Remember those letters and words you've learned. You'll need them."

Keep up the good work!

Sincerely,
The Authors

Unit 4 Contents

Let's Go Exploring

Where will our adventures take us?

4

Week 2

Unit 4 Contents

Don Leu
The Internet Guy

Right before our eyes, the nature of reading and learning is changing. The Internet and other technologies create new opportunities, new solutions, and new literacies. New reading comprehension skills are required online. They are increasingly important to our students and our society.

Those of us on the Reading Street team are here to help you on this new, and very exciting, journey.

See It!

- Big Question Video

- Concept Talk Video

- Envision It! Animations

- eReaders

Hear It!

- *Sing with Me* **Animations**

- eSelections

- Grammar Jammer

Adam and Kim **play at the beach.**

Concept Talk Video

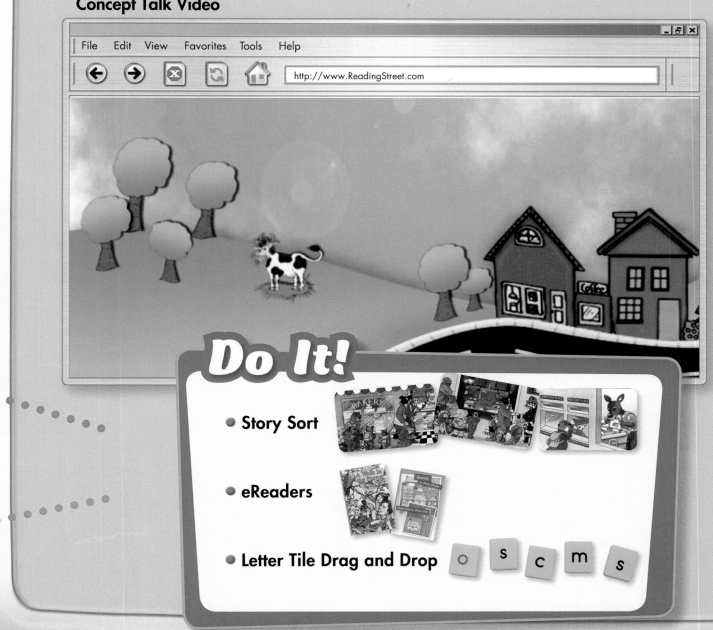

File Edit View Favorites Tools Help

http://www.ReadingStreet.com

Do It!

- **Story Sort**

- **eReaders**

- **Letter Tile Drag and Drop** o s c m s

Let's Go Exploring

THE BIG Q

Where will our adventures take us?

Objectives
• Point out groups of spoken words that begin with the same sound.
• Blend a beginning sound with the vowel sound and what follows it to make simple words. • Say the sound at the beginning of spoken one-syllable words.

Let's Listen for

Initial Sounds

● Point to a hand. Say the word. Say the beginning sound.

■ Find three things that begin with /h/, like *hand*.

▲ Point to these pictures and say the words: *hanger, hippo, hair.* Do they begin the same? What about *shoe, leg, house?*

★ Point to the hat. Say /h/ -*at*. Blend the word. Change /h/ to /b/. Blend the new word.

Read Together

READING STREET ONLINE
BIG QUESTION VIDEO
www.ReadingStreet.com

12

Objectives
● Describe the events of a story in order.

Comprehension

Envision It!

Sequence

**READING STREET ONLINE
ENVISION IT! ANIMATIONS**
www.ReadingStreet.com

14

Objectives

● Point out the common sounds that letters stand for. ● Use what you know about letters and their sounds to read words in a list and in sentences or stories. ● Know and read at least 25 often-used words.

Hh

helicopter

READING STREET ONLINE
ALPHABET CARDS
www.ReadingStreet.com

Phonics

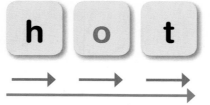 **Initial** *Hh*

Words I Can Blend

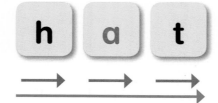

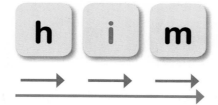

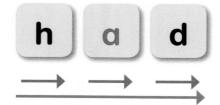

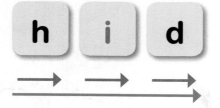

Words I Can Read

are

that

do

Sentences I Can Read

1. They are hot.

2. That hat is for him.

3. Do you like the hat?

Objectives
● Point out the common sounds that letters stand for. ● Use what you know about letters and their sounds to read words in a list and in sentences or stories. ● Know and read at least 25 often-used words.

Phonics

I Can Read!

Decodable Reader

● Consonant *Hh*
   Hob
   hit
   hot
   had
   hat

■ High-Frequency Words
   that
   is
   do
   see
   a
   they
   are

▲ Read the story.

READING STREET ONLINE
DECODABLE eREADERS
www.ReadingStreet.com

Hob Can Hit

Written by Roy Kass
Illustrated by Ryan Bines

Decodable Reader 19

That man is Dan Hob.
Hob can hit.
Hob can do it!

That fan is Pam.
Can Pam see Hob?
Pam can.

That fan is Sam.
Can Sam see Hob?
Sam can.

Did Hob hit it?
Hob did not.

Did Hob hit it?
Hob did not.

Hob is hot.
Hob had a hat.

Pop! Hob hit it!
Hob did it!
They are not sad.

Envision It! Retell

Rooster's Off to See the World

Big Book

1

2

3

4

5

6

READING STREET ONLINE
STORY SORT
www.ReadingStreet.com

26

Think, Talk, and Write

1. Would you choose to see the world with Rooster? Why or why not? Text to Self

2. What does Rooster do first in the story? What does he do last?

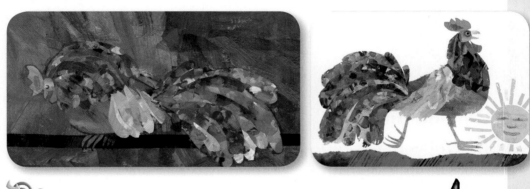

Sequence

3. Look back and write.

27

Objectives

● Identify and put pictures of objects into groups. ● Listen closely to speakers by facing them and asking questions to help you better understand the information. ● Follow directions said aloud that have a short list of actions.

Let's Learn It!

Vocabulary

● Talk about the pictures.

■ What did you do before school?

▲ What will you do after school?

★ Form a line. Who is at the beginning of the line? Who is at the end?

Listening and Speaking

● Point to AlphaBuddy's nose.

■ Point to AlphaBuddy's mouth.

▲ Point to AlphaBuddy's ear.

★ Point to AlphaBuddy's foot.

Vocabulary

Sequence Words

before

after

beginning

end

28

Give Directions

Be a good speaker!

Objectives
● Ask and answer questions about texts read aloud. ● Point out the phrases and characters that appear in many different stories from around the world. ● Discuss the reasons for reading and listening to different kinds of texts.

Let's Practice It!

Lullaby

● Listen to the lullaby.

■ Which lines repeat?

▲ What animals are mentioned in this lullaby? What are they doing?

★ What is the purpose of a lullaby? How does a lullaby do that?

Objectives

● Point out groups of spoken words that begin with the same sound.
● Blend a beginning sound with the vowel sound and what follows it to make simple words. ● Say the sound at the beginning of spoken one-syllable words.

Phonemic Awareness

Let's Listen for

Initial Sounds

Read Together

● Point to the loaf of bread. Say *loaf*. Say the beginning sound.

■ Point to the bell. Say *bell*. Say the ending sound.

▲ Find three things that begin with /l/. Find three things that end with /l/.

★ Point to these things and say the words: *leg, lid, lap.* Do they begin the same? Do these words end the same: *girl, fill, doll?*

♥ Blend /f/ -ill. What is the word? Yes, *fill*. Change /f/ to /w/. Blend the new word.

33

Objectives
● Identify what happens in a text and why it happens.

Comprehension

Envision It!

Cause and Effect

READING STREET ONLINE
ENVISION IT! ANIMATIONS
www.ReadingStreet.com

Ll

lemon

READING STREET ONLINE
ALPHABET CARDS
www.ReadingStreet.com

Phonics

Initial and Final *Ll*

Words I Can Blend

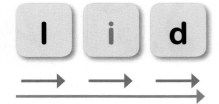

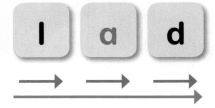

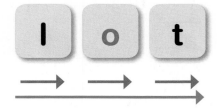

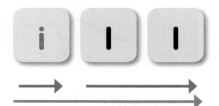

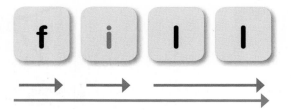

Words I Can Read

are

that

do

Sentences I Can Read

1. That man is my dad.
2. We are on the hill.
3. Do you hop a lot?

Objectives
● Point out the common sounds that letters stand for. ● Use what you know about letters and their sounds to read words in a list and in sentences or stories. ● Know and read at least 25 often-used words.

Phonics

I Can Read!

Decodable Reader

● Consonant *Ll*
lap
Lil
lit
doll
lid

■ High-Frequency Words

a	do
you	see
the	they
that	are

▲ Read the story.

READING STREET ONLINE
DECODABLE eREADERS
www.ReadingStreet.com

Can It Fit?

Written by Myleen Rush
Illustrated by Gloria Leek

Decodable Reader 20

Tab sat on a lap.
Kit did not.

Lil lit it.
Do you see Tab?

Lil had a doll.
Kit can bat it.

Kit sat in the lid.
Can Tab fit?

They fit in that lid.

Can Tab fit on Lil?
Can Kit fit on Lil?

They are on Lil.

Objectives
• Tell in your own words a main event from a story read aloud. • Describe characters in a story and why they act the way they do. • Retell or act out important events of a story.

Envision It! | Retell

Trade Book

1

2

3

4

5

6

READING STREET ONLINE
STORY SORT
www.ReadingStreet.com

46

Think, Talk, and Write

1. Tell about a lucky
adventure you have had.

Text to Self

2. What does the fox do to
the piglet? Why does he
do this?

Cause and Effect

3. Look back and write.

Vocabulary

● Talk about the pictures.

■ Find things that are fuzzy.

▲ Find things that are bumpy.

★ Find things that are furry.

♥ Find things that are sharp.

Listening and Speaking

● How are breakfast and dinner alike?

■ How are breakfast and dinner different?

▲ How are a pig and a fox alike?

★ How are a pig and a fox different?

Vocabulary

Words for Textures

fuzzy

bumpy

sharp

furry

48

Compare and Contrast

Be a good listener!

Get Ready For Grade 1

Let's
Practice
It!

Fable

● Listen to the fable.

■ Why can't the crow get the water in the pitcher?

▲ Why does the crow drop pebbles into the pitcher?

★ What lesson does the fable teach?

♥ What new expression does this fable teach you?

● When have you done something a little at a time? Tell about it.

The Crow and the Pitcher

1

2

50

51

Objectives

- Point out groups of spoken words that begin with the same sound.
- Blend a beginning sound with the vowel sound and what follows it to make simple words.

Phonemic Awareness

Let's Listen for

Read Together

Initial Sounds

● Point to a sled. Say *sled*. Say the blended sound at the beginning: /s/ /l/, /sl/.

■ Point to the plow. Say *plow*. Say the blended sound at the beginning: /p/ /l/, /pl/.

▲ Find things that begin with /sl/, /pl/, /bl/, /gl/, /fl/.

★ Say these words: *spin, spell, speak*. Do they begin the same? What about *crack, crash, skate?*

♥ Blend /sl/ -*ip*. What's the word? Yes, *slip*. Change /sl/ to /kl/ to blend a new word.

READING STREET ONLINE
BIG QUESTION VIDEO
www.ReadingStreet.com

52

Comprehension

Envision It!

Sequence

READING STREET ONLINE
ENVISION IT! ANIMATIONS
www.ReadingStreet.com

55

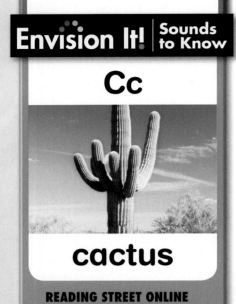

Envision It! | Sounds to Know

Cc

cactus

Phonics

Consonant Blends

Words I Can Blend

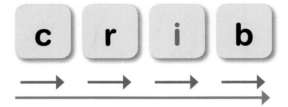

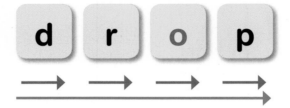

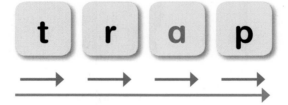

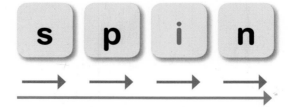

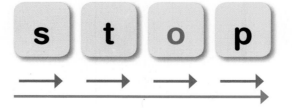

Words I Can Read

one

two

three

four

five

Sentences I Can Read

1. One pal can spin.
2. Two can snap.
3. Can three flop?
4. I see four tots.
5. Can you do five flips?

57

Phonics

I Can Read!

Decodable Reader

● Consonant Blends

flop	spin
slam	land
drop	jump
plop	stop

■ High-Frequency Words

a
one
two
three
four
five

▲ Read the story.

READING STREET ONLINE
DECODABLE eREADERS
www.ReadingStreet.com

One to Five

Written by Heather Leavy
Illustrated by Kris Pool

Decodable Reader 21

SPIN!

One sat on a mat.
Flop!

Two ran on a pan.
Spin! Spin!

Three hid in a lid.
Slam! Slam! Slam!

Four land on a lap.
Drop! Drop! Drop! Drop!

Five jump on top.
Plop! Plop! Plop! Plop! Plop!

Flop! Spin! Slam! Drop! Plop!

Stop! Stop! Stop!

Objectives
● Tell in your own words a main event from a story read aloud. ● Retell or act out important events of a story. ● Connect what you read to other things you have read or heard. ● Describe the events of a story in order.

Envision It! | Retell

Big Book

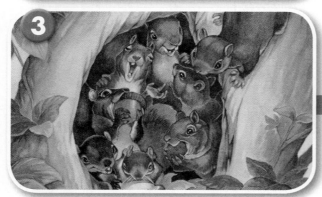

READING STREET ONLINE
STORY SORT
www.ReadingStreet.com

Think, Talk, and Write

1. How is Rooster's adventure like Little Mouse's adventure? How are they different?

Text to Text

2. What happens first in the story? What happens last?

Sequence

3. Look back and write.

Vocabulary

- Where might you see heart shapes?
- Look around for star shapes.
- What do you see that has an oval shape?
- What do you see that has a diamond shape?
- Which shape is your favorite?

Listening and Speaking

- What happens first in the story?
- What happens next in the story?
- Then what happens in the story?
- What happens last in the story?

Vocabulary

Words for Shapes

heart

star

oval

diamond

Listen for Sequence

Be a good listener!

Objectives
● Tell what an informational story read aloud was about. ● Follow directions with pictures. ● Use the cover, title, illustrations, and plot to make a guess about things that the author does not tell you. ● Connect what you read to your own experiences.

Make a Kazoo!

Let's Practice It!

Directions

● Listen to the directions.

■ What do the directions tell about?

▲ What is the second step?

★ What does the boy think of his kazoo? How do you know?

♥ Tell about something you made. What did you use? What did you do?

Step 1

Step 2

Step 3

Step 4

71

Objectives
- Point out groups of spoken words that begin with the same sound.
- Blend a beginning sound with the vowel sound and what follows it to make simple words. • Say the sound at the beginning of spoken one-syllable words.

Let's Listen for

Initial Sounds

Read Together

● Point to the gate. Say the word. Say the beginning sound.

■ Find three things that begin with /g/, like *gate*.

▲ Say these words: *ball, grape, field*. Do they begin with the same sound? What about *game, gate, goal*?

★ Blend /g/ -ate. What's the word? Yes, *gate*. Change /g/ to /l/ and blend a new word.

READING STREET ONLINE
BIG QUESTION VIDEO
www.ReadingStreet.com

72

Objectives
● Point out parts of a story including where it takes place, the characters, and the main events. ● Describe characters in a story and why they act the way they do.

Comprehension

Envision It!

Literary Elements

READING STREET ONLINE
ENVISION IT! ANIMATIONS
www.ReadingStreet.com

Characters

Setting

Plot

75

Objectives

• Use what you know about letters and their sounds to read words in a list and in sentences or stories.
• Notice that new words are made when letters are changed, added, or taken away.

Envision It! | **Sounds to Know**

Gg

goose

READING STREET ONLINE
ALPHABET CARDS
www.ReadingStreet.com

Phonics

Initial *Gg*

Words I Can Blend

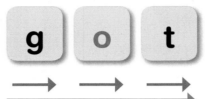

g o t

g a s

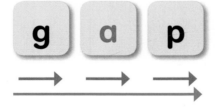

g a p

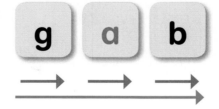

g a b

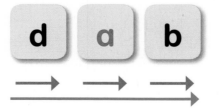

d a b

Words I Can Read

one

two

three

four

five

Sentences I Can Read

1. We can grab one bat.

2. Two hits land on the grass!

3. Brad got three hits.

4. Gil got four hits.

5. Gram can clap five claps.

Phonics

I Can Read!

Decodable Reader

● Consonant *Gg*
Gil
got
flag

■ High-Frequency Words
one
two
three
four
five
a
is

▲ Read the story.

READING STREET ONLINE
DECODABLE eREADERS
www.ReadingStreet.com

Gil Got One

Decodable Reader 22

Written by William Dillberts
Illustrated by Hillary Gem

Gil got one.
Pop!
Sad Gil.

Gil got two.
Pop! Pop!
Sad Gil.

Gil got three.
Pop! Pop! Pop!
Sad Gil.

Gil got four.
Pop! Pop! Pop! Pop!
Sad Gil.

Gil got five.
Pop! Pop! Pop! Pop! Pop!
Sad Gil.

Mom had a plan.
Mom got Gil a flag.

Gil is not sad.

Envision It! Retell

Trade Book

Think, Talk, and Write

1. What do you think Goldilocks learned? Text to World

2. Which is a character from *Goldilocks and the Three Bears?*

 Character

3. Look back and write.

87

Objectives
● Understand that compound words are made up of shorter words.
● Share information and ideas by speaking clearly and using proper language.

Let's Learn It!

Vocabulary

● Talk about the pictures.

■ Blend the words *bed* and *room*.

▲ Segment the word *tiptoe*.

Listening and Speaking

● Would you rather be an author or an illustrator? Tell why.

Vocabulary

Compound Words

bed + room =

bedroom

 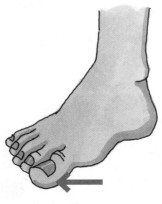 

tip + toe = tiptoe

Discuss Authors and Illustrators

title

author

illustrator

Be a good speaker!

Objectives
● Point out parts of a story including where it takes place. ● Discuss the big idea, or *theme,* of a folk tale or fable and connect it to your own life.
● Point out the phrases and characters that appear in many different stories from around the world.

How the Fly Saved the River

Let's Practice It!

Folk Tale

● Listen to the folk tale.

■ How does the story begin?

▲ When and where does the story take place?

★ How are these characters like the ones in "The Three Little Pigs"?

♥ What lesson does the folk tale teach? Share ideas about how the lesson can help you.

90

91

Objectives
- Point out groups of spoken words that begin with the same sound.
- Say the sound at the beginning of spoken one-syllable words.

Let's Listen for

Read Together

Initial Sounds

● Say *Ed*. What sound do you hear at the beginning of *Ed*?

■ Find three things that begin with /e/, like *Ed*.

▲ Name other words that begin with /e/.

★ Say these words: *Ed, elm, engine*. Do they begin the same? What about *end, clown, egg*?

READING STREET ONLINE
BIG QUESTION VIDEO
www.ReadingStreet.com

DINER

92

93

Comprehension

Envision It!

Classify and Categorize

READING STREET ONLINE
ENVISION IT! ANIMATIONS
www.ReadingStreet.com

Envision It! | Sounds to Know

Ee

escalator

READING STREET ONLINE
ALPHABET CARDS
www.ReadingStreet.com

Phonics

Short *e*

Words I Can Blend

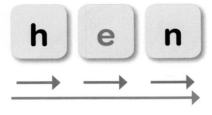

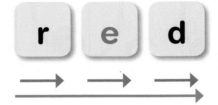

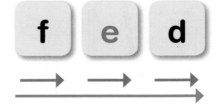

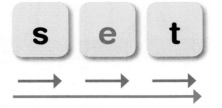

Words I Can Read

here

go

from

Sentences I Can Read

1. Ben is here.

2. We go to see Meg.

3. The hen is from Meg.

Objectives
● Point out the common sounds that letters stand for. ● Use what you know about letters and their sounds to read words in a list and in sentences or stories. ● Know and read at least 25 often-used words.

Phonics

I Can Read!

Decodable Reader

● Short *Ee*

get	Red
Hen	Ben
pen	Ken
Len	

■ High-Frequency Words
go
the
from
here

▲ Read the story.

Decodable Reader 23

Red Hen

Written by Nathan Aguilera
Illustrated by Samantha Johnson

Get Red Hen, Ben.
Red Hen can go in the pen.

Red Hen ran from Ben.
Red Hen hid here.

Red Hen did not get in the pen.

Get Red Hen, Ken.
Red Hen can go in the pen.

Red Hen ran from Ken.
Red Hen hid here.

Red Hen did not get in the pen.

Len got Red Hen!

Objectives

- Retell the important facts from a selection heard or read.
- Connect what you read to your own experiences, to other things you have read or heard, and to the world around you.

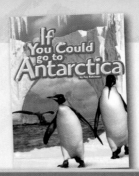

Big Book

Envision It! | Retell

1

2

3

4

5

6

Think, Talk, and Write

1. What would you like to do on an Antarctic adventure? Text to Self

2. Which does not belong in Antarctica?

Classify and Categorize

3. Look back and write.

Objectives
• Understand and use new words that name actions, directions, positions, the order of something, and places.
• Listen closely to speakers by facing them and asking questions to help you better understand the information.

Vocabulary

● Talk about the pictures.

■ Point to north on the map.

▲ Now point to south, east, and west.

Listening and Speaking

● Name the characters in the stories.

Vocabulary

Direction Words

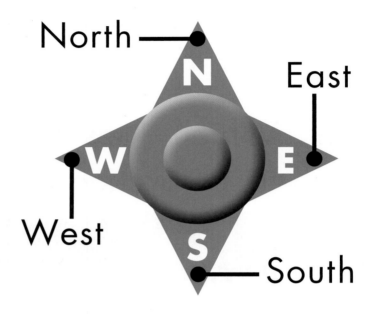

North

East

West

South

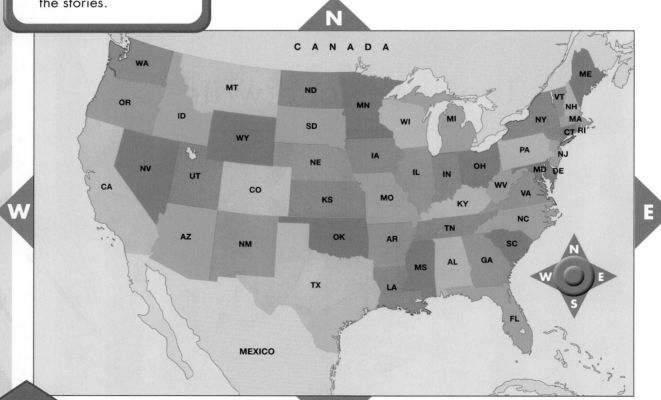

Listen for Story Elements
Character

Be a good
listener!

One, Two, Buckle My Shoe

Let's Practice It!

Nursery Rhyme

● Listen to the rhyme.

■ Say the rhyme. Clap your hands to show each beat.

▲ Which words rhyme? Name another word that rhymes with each pair.

★ Why do children like to read and listen to nursery rhymes?

1 2

Mail

3
4

5 6

7 8

9

10

Objectives
● Blend a beginning sound with the vowel sound and what follows it to make simple words. ● Say the sound at the beginning of spoken one-syllable words.

Let's Listen for

Initial Sounds

Read Together

● Say the sound you hear at the beginning of *elephant, hat, leaf, girl, flag, star, crowd.*

■ Point to the elephant. Find something that begins like *elephant.*

▲ Now find pictures that begin with /h/, /l/, /g/, /fl/, /st/, and /kr/.

★ Name other words that begin with /e/, /h/, /l/, /g/, /fl/, /st/, and /kr/.

♥ Blend /h/ -at. What's the word? Yes, *hat.* Now change /h/ to /fl/ to make a new word.

READING STREET ONLINE
BIG QUESTION VIDEO
www.ReadingStreet.com

112

Objectives

• Point out parts of a story including where it takes place, the characters, and the main events.

Comprehension

Envision It!

Literary Elements

READING STREET ONLINE
ENVISION IT! ANIMATIONS
www.ReadingStreet.com

Characters

Setting

Plot

115

Objectives
- Use what you know about letters and their sounds to read words in a list and in sentences or stories.
- Notice that new words are made when letters are changed, added, or taken away.

Envision It! | **Sounds to Know**

Ee

escalator

READING STREET ONLINE
ALPHABET CARDS
www.ReadingStreet.com

Phonics

Short e

Words I Can Blend

b e d

r e d

f e d

f e l l

t e l l

Words I Can Read

here

go

from

Sentences I Can Read

1. My dad is here.
2. I go to help him.
3. The pen is from Mom.

Objectives
● Point out the common sounds that letters stand for. ● Use what you know about letters and their sounds to read words in a list and in sentences or stories. ● Know and read at least 25 often-used words.

Phonics

I Can Read!

Decodable Reader

● Short *Ee*

Peg	met
Ned	pet
Hen	pen
bed	get
fed	let

■ High-Frequency Words

a
from
here
is
have
go

▲ Read the story.

A Pet Hen

Written by Fran Quinn
Illustrated by Jason Edwards

Decodable Reader 24

Peg met Ned.
Peg got a pet from Ned.
Here is Hen.

Did Hen have a pen?
Hen did not.

Peg got Hen a pen.
Go in, Hen.

Did Hen have a bed?
Hen did not.

Peg got Hen a bed.
Get in, Hen.

Peg fed Hen.

Peg got in bed.
Let Peg nap, Hen.

Objectives

• Point out parts of a story including where it takes place. • Tell in your own words a main event from a story read aloud. • Retell or act out important events of a story. • Connect what you read to the world around you.

Envision It! Retell

Trade Book

READING STREET ONLINE
STORY SORT
www.ReadingStreet.com

126

Think, Talk, and Write

1. Why is Rosalba and Abuela's adventure special? How can others have such an adventure? Text to World

2. Where does the story *Abuela* take place?

Setting

3. Look back and write.

127

Objectives
● Listen closely to speakers by facing them and asking questions to help you better understand the information.
● Follow rules for discussions, including taking turns and speaking one at a time.

Vocabulary

● Talk about the picture.

■ What day of the week is it today?

▲ In what month is your birthday?

Listening and Speaking

● Say some words from a poem, song, or nursery rhyme.

Vocabulary

Time Words

Month

March

Day

Week

Sunday	Monday	Tuesday	Wednesday	Thursday	Friday	Saturday
		1	2	3	4	5
6	7	8	9	10	11	12
13	14	15	16	17	18	19
20	21	22	23	24	25	26
27	28	29	30	31		

128

Listen to Poems

Be a good listener!

Let's Practice It!

Expository Text

● Listen to the selection. What is it about?

■ Who gave the statue to the people of the United States?

▲ What information did the author tell about first? next? and last?

★ What details, or special facts, does the author tell us about what the statue looks like?

♥ What questions does the selection make you want to ask?

The Statue of Liberty

1

Words for Things That Go

airplane

bike

truck

car

bus

van

boat

train

Words for Colors

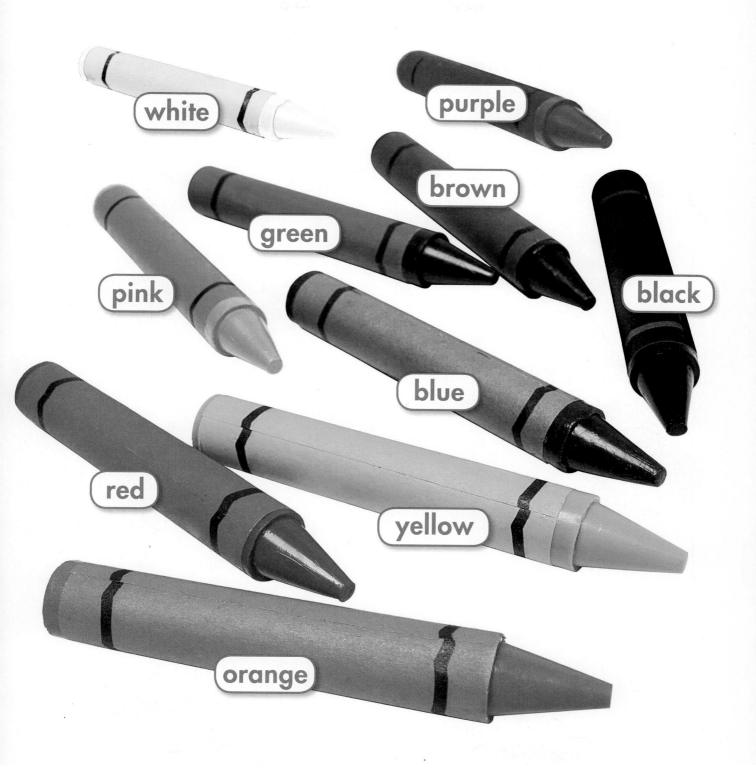

white

purple

green

brown

pink

blue

black

red

yellow

orange

Words for Shapes

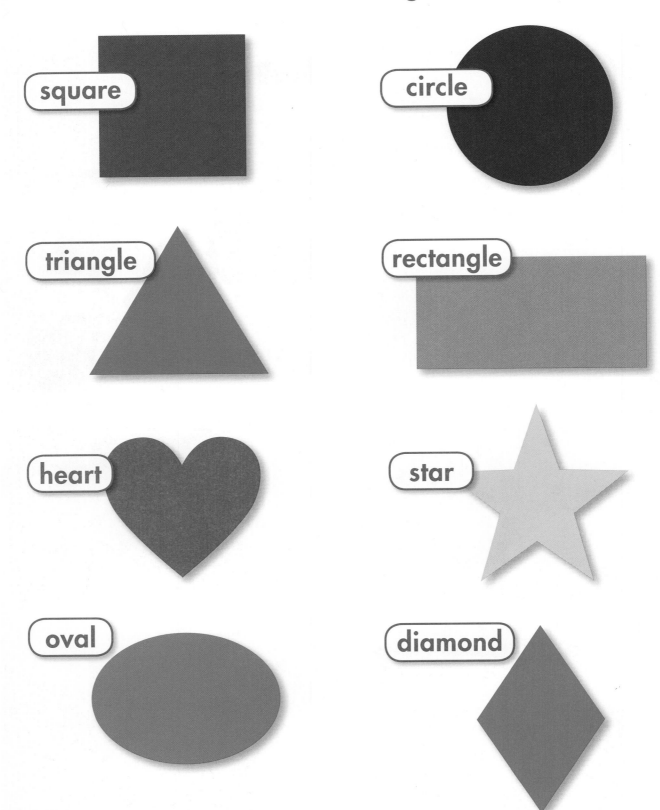

square

circle

triangle

rectangle

heart

star

oval

diamond

Words for Places

school

home

park

train station

police station

fire station

post office

library

Words for Animals

lion

mouse

puppy

dog

cat

kitten

duck

turtle

chick

hen

rooster

bird

butterfly

fish

whale

bear

panda

caterpillar

beaver

calf

cow

Words for Actions

skip

walk

run

fly

swim

ride

jump

hop

138

Position Words

up

in

out

down

on

around

over

under

My Classroom

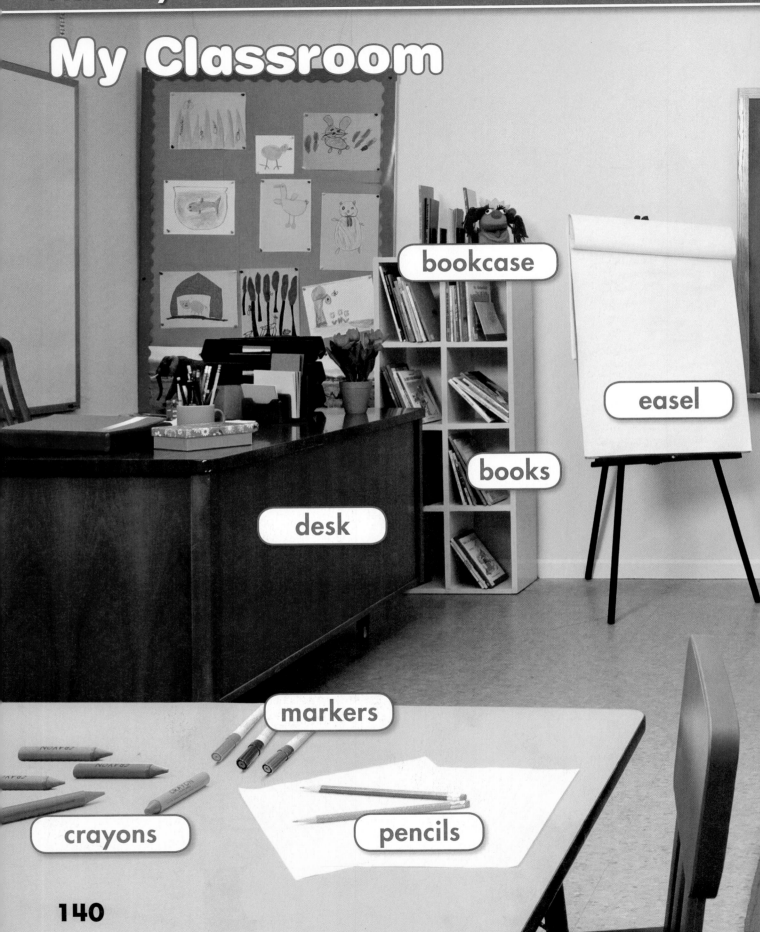

bookcase

easel

books

desk

markers

crayons

pencils

teacher

toys

paper

chair

blocks

table

rug

Words for Feelings

happy

frightened

worried

excited

angry

proud

sad

surprised

My Family

mom
mother

dad
father

sister

grandmother

grandfather

brother

Acknowledgments

Illustrations

Cover: Rob Hefferan

12 Manja Stojic

19–25 Cale Atkinson

28, 49, 69, 88, 129 George Ulrich

30 Jan Bryan Hunt

32 Aaron Zenz

39–45 Natalia Vasquez

50–51 Steve Mack

52 Marilyn Janovitz

59–65 Dani Jones

72 Steve Simpson

90–91 Jason Wolff

92 Ron Lieser

99–105 Robbie Short

110–111 Vanessa Newton

112 Karol Kaminski

119–125 Wednesday Kirwan.

Photographs

Every effort has been made to secure permission and provide appropriate credit for photographic material. The publisher deeply regrets any omission and pledges to correct errors called to its attention in subsequent editions.

Unless otherwise acknowledged, all photographs are the property of Pearson Education, Inc.

Photo locators denoted as follows: Top (T), Center (C), Bottom (B), Left (L), Right (R), Background (Bkgd)

10 (B) ©Mario Lopes/Alamy

48 ©Andy Sands/Nature Picture Library, ©Envision/Corbis, ©Fusion Pix/Corbis, Dave King/©DK Images

130 (B) ©Thinkstock/Corbis

131 (C) ©Jochen Tack/Peter Arnold, Inc., (T, B) ©Peter Bennett/Ambient Images, Inc., (TL) PhotoLibrary Group, Ltd.